Discovers Every Bird is Beautiful

Written by Angie Bird & Eva Vandenbergh
Illustrated by Lillian Jones

HIGHLANDER PRESS

GLITTER BIRD

Copyright © 2022 by Angie Bird
Illustrations Copyright © 2022 by Lillian Jones

All rights reserved. The contents of this book may not be transmitted or reproduced in any form or by any means, mechanical or electronic, including photocopying, recording or by any information storage and retrieval system, without prior written permission from the author, with the exception only of the inclusion of brief quotations in a review.

Limit of Liability Disclaimer: The contents of this book are intended for information purposes only and may not apply to your individual situation. The author, publisher, and distributor in no way guarantee the accuracy of the contents. The information is subjective and should be treated as such when reviewing the contents. Neither the Publisher nor the author shall be liable for any loss of profit or any other commercial damages resulting from actions taken based on the contents of this guide. All links contained in this book are for information purposes only and are not warranted for content, accuracy, or any other implied or explicit purpose.

ISBN: 978-1-956442-04-5
Library of Congress Control Number: 2022937271

Published by Highlander Press
501 W. University Pkwy, Ste. B2
Baltimore, MD 21210

Cover design: Lillian Jones
Interior Layout: Catherine Williams
Editor: Deborah Kevin, MA

Printed in the United States of America

*You are amazing, beautiful, and deserving
of love exactly how you are in this moment.*
~Angie Bird

Be your own way. Fly your own way.
~Eva Vandenbergh

You'll find birds in every sky

and all across the land.

All have feathers.

Each came from an egg.

Some birds are green.

Some are blue.

Some are short.

Some are tall.

Some are big.

Some are small.

Some birds fly, others run,

some swim.

Some birds have long beaks.

Some have short beaks.

Some birds talk.

Some birds sing.

Some birds hunt.

Some birds have feeders.

Some are love birds.

Some are night owls.

Others are early birds.

Every bird is beautiful.
Each has something to offer the world.

People are like that too.
Everyone is beautiful in their own way.

Embrace your beauty.

Reasons I am AMAZING!

Write 10 things about yourself that are amazing.
Keep this list as a reminder, if you ever feel down.

1.
2.
3.
4.
5.
6.
7.
8.
9.
10.

Bullying Resources
Find out how you can help stop bullying. **www.stopbullying.gov**
Are you a bully? Take the quiz. **www.pacerkidsagainstbullying.org**
Need to talk with someone confidentially? **Text HELLO to 741741**

About the Birds in this Book
Glitter Bird is based on a dove. Doves bring peace and hope to hurting hearts. Doves belong to those whose gentle compassion heal the world. Glitter Bird's mom is flying to see her on page 4.

Page	Type of Bird	IUCN Red List Category
2	Lesser Flamingo	Near Threatened
2	Black Crowned Crane	Vulnerable
2	Secretary Bird	Vulnerable
3	Yellow Billed Hornbill	Least Concern
6	Guinea Turaco	Least Concern
7	Blue Bellied Roller	Least Concern
8	Brown Kiwi	Vulnerable
9	Somali Ostrich	Vulnerable
10	Harpy Eagle	Near Threatened
11	Anna's Hummingbird	Least Concern
12	Tristan Albatross	Critically Endangered
12	Lesser Roadrunner	Least Concern
13	Flightless Cormorant	Vulnerable
14	Keel Billed Toucan	Least Concern
15	Owl Finch	Least Concern
16	Grey Parrot	Endangered

17	Budgies/Parakeets	Least Concern
18	Harris Hawk	Least Concern
19	Cardinal and Blue Jay	Least Concern
21	Magnificent Frigate Bird	Least Concern
22	Long Eared Owl	Least Concern
23	Chicken	Least Concern

The International Union for Conservation of Nature (IUCN) Red List is the world's most comprehensive inventory of the conservation status of the world's species.
A portion of this book's proceeds support the World Bird Sanctuary. Learn more at **www.WorldBirdSanctuary.org**

About the Authors

Angie Bird and Eva Vandenbergh are a mother/daughter duo who faced a challenge of the bathroom bullies and decided to turn it into a story of a delightful myriad of birds. They love to travel, learn and share their inspiration with others. They hope you grow from your challenges and see yourself as beautiful and amazing. They bird watch in Memphis, TN. Follow on Facebook @AngieGlitterBird.

About the Illustrator

Lillian Jones is a freelance artist, furry and animal enthusiast. She has seen the harmful effects of bullying and she rises as a champion against it. She loves birds and all animals and works to increase awareness and protection for at risk species. Follow her on Instagram @Lemurskii.

About the Publisher

Highlander Press, founded in 2019, is a mid-sized publishing company committed to diversity and sharing big ideas thereby changing the world through words. What makes Highlander Press unique is that their business model focuses on building strong collaborative relationships with other women-owned businesses, which specialize in some aspect of the publishing industry, such as graphic design, book marketing, book launching, copyrights, and publicity. The mantra "a rising tide lifts all boats" is one they embrace. Follow them on Instagram @HighlanderPress or their website at **https://highlanderpressbooks.com**.

CPSIA information can be obtained
at www.ICGtesting.com
Printed in the USA
LVHW070832040622
720490LV00002B/2